EMPOWERED
2022

REKINDLE THE FLAME

Edited By Debbie Killingworth

First published in Great Britain in 2022 by:

Young Writers
Remus House
Coltsfoot Drive
Peterborough
PE2 9BF
Telephone: 01733 890066
Website: www.youngwriters.co.uk

Book Design by Ashley Janson

Softback ISBN 978-1-83928-624-7

Printed and bound in the UK by BookPrintingUK
Website: www.bookprintinguk.com
YB0520B

☆ FOREWORD ☆

Since 1991, here at Young Writers we have celebrated the awesome power of creative writing, especially in young adults where it can serve as a vital method of expressing their emotions and views about the world around them. In every poem we see the effort and thought that each student published in this book has put into their work and by creating this anthology we hope to encourage them further with the ultimate goal of sparking a life-long love of writing.

Our latest competition for secondary school students, Empowered, challenged young writers to consider what was important to them. We wanted to give them a voice, the chance to express themselves freely and honestly, something which is so important for these young adults to feel confident and listened to. They could give an opinion, share a memory, consider a dilemma, impart advice or simply write about something they love. There were no restrictions on style or subject so you will find an anthology brimming with a variety of poetic styles and topics. We hope you find it as absorbing as we have.

We encourage young writers to express themselves and address subjects that matter to them, which sometimes means writing about sensitive or contentious topics. If you have been affected by any issues raised in this book, details on where to find help can be found at www.youngwriters.co.uk/info/other/contact-lines

CONTENTS

THE POEMS

Self-Love

See yourself as others see you,
You are kind, you are nice and beautiful too,
You're amazing, you should know it's true,
Love yourself, you are so cool
And here is a poem to tell you that too.

Are you part of the LGBTQ?
Understand that that is you,
You don't need what's on the news
To help you with what you choose.

You could be religious
Or sporty and weird,
But all of these things just make you unique,
Unique is what you are,
Just be proud of all your scars.

You should know that what you look like,
Who you are or what you do,
You are perfect just the way you are,
Please believe that because it's true.

You are amazing and self-love is important,
So look at yourself in a mirror and just smile,
And remember that you are worth it,
You should believe it, because you are.

Caitlin Trickett (12)
Castleford Academy, Castleford

Time Is Precious

Time is unbeatable in value,
There is no simile that may suffice,
As a comparison of the worth of time,
Is like seeing a pig fly,
There is nothing that clutches more merit in its moving hands,
Than the terrific trickling time that many may desire.

Yet yearning for it serves no purpose,
As there is a limit, we all possess,
Like a battery on a watch,
When will it end?
This restriction is unable to be altered,
Thus, we must make the best of our gift,
We must make it our quest.

The feeling of your past is irrelevant,
Worry about the future is even more,
What does matter is the present,
A gift,
That you must adore,
As the turning of the clock is ineffectual,
The dwelling,
You cannot afford.

We all know that life has a start and end,
The truth is, it is the middle that counts,

What you do with your gift of time,
The ticking seconds, minutes, hours,
Is not up to anyone but yourself.

'Be yourself, everyone else is taken' said Oscar Wilde,
I believe it was said in hope to educate,
He knew the true meaning of life,
To enjoy rather than to debate.
As to be 'regular' like the sudden movements of time,
Is to lack the sense of joyfulness of the turning cogs inside.

Contrarily it is okay to cry,
For the clock to be fast,
It is part of human nature,
To spill it all out,
To confide.

It shall reward you greatly as in the long run,
The tower shall ring,
Your gift,
Your present shall be improved,
Because of your seemingly,
'Terrible news'.

Due to your greatness,
Your faults seem so hideous,
How you should not torture yourself,
Rather, talk to yourself.

Remember that your thoughts provide you,
Your movements that guide you,
But in the end,
It is your actions that define you.

Your past may have not gone as planned,
But life is a mysterious, magical roller coaster that is not in our hands,
Who knows when the clocks will go forward?
To fail is to succeed,
We cannot grow nor evolve without those mistakes,
Therefore, you should not stereotype yourself with those errors,
As in the end,
Your faults were your aid in life,
You are who you are because of them.

Intrusive those thoughts you have may be,
The anxiety,
Tick-tock, tick-tock, tick-tock,
The guilt,
It can happen to you or me.

Your mind may have fallen ill,
Your mind is a patient in a hospital,
Like the ear-splitting sonorous sound of an alarm clock,
Encapturing your mind,
Your mind may be captured,
Stuck in a seemingly endless loop of pain and suffering,

No medicine works for your mind,
Maybe you would do anything for it to end,
Maybe you are prepared to make the jump and let it all go,
And to your mind I say,
I do not know you,
Your situation,
Where you work,
But do not make the jump,
Rather tell others,
Reward yourself,
Get more sleep,
Focus on the positives,
This time, hopefully, your mind may be out of the hospital,
And calm like the gentle ticks of a clock.

Nevertheless, you can feel empowered,
You will be strong, happy, confident,
You can win and be yourself,
Be who you want to be.

Fight those thoughts,
Or you will begin to forget,
What you need to remember,
That everything is okay.

Your achievements and those who are close,
The great time you spent,
Your greatest and most precious perfect present,
How you should make the most of it all as you cannot get any more.

Stand up, smile,
You deserve that wealth,
Talk to people,
Have fun,
But most importantly enjoy yourself.

Now you have reached the end of my long poem,
Was it worth your time?
Have you enjoyed yourself?
Been interested?
Learnt something?

Or is this going to be a forgotten memory of yours,
Forever lost in time?
Just remember...
'Time is the most valuable thing a man can spend' -
Theophrastus.

Adam Davies (12)
Castleford Academy, Castleford

Learn To Love Yourself

When you look in the mirror,
Tell me, what do you see?
Do you see yourself as a stranger,
Or do you proudly look and think, *that's me?*
Can you smile at your reflection,
Or do you slowly pull it apart?
Don't let your eyes do the talking,
Look at yourself with your heart.
You don't need to try to be perfect,
Because perfect doesn't exist.
When being kind to others,
Make sure you're on that list.
You know that you're still growing,
That your body and looks will change.
Try to be friends with the future you,
Even though it may seem strange.
The person in the mirror is looking right back at you,
Tell them they are amazing
And just be the beautiful you.

Lexi Robinson (12)
Castleford Academy, Castleford

Perfect

When boredom hits you
Social media comes to the rescue
You start scrolling through these images
Seeing these perfect appearances.

I stare at my body
All I want is to be like the people online
I stare in front of the mirror
And the glass shatters
Shards pierce my skin
Striking my self-esteem.

Too fat, too thin,
Too spotty, too plain,
It's okay to not be okay.

I see myself,
No one else can be me
My size, my shape is perfect
It's not important how you look
It's how it makes you feel
Why would you want to be someone else
When you can be yourself?

It's like beautiful doesn't even exist
Unless you can cross everything off the checklist
You are not devalued

Even if the woman next to you looks perfect
You are always a value
If you value you.

Maisie Clarkson (12)
Castleford Academy, Castleford

Empowered

Don't give up,
You can do it,
You have people around you
To help you through it.

Your mum, brother, sister or dad,
They will help you through it,
When you do bad.

You have people around you,
Nearly everywhere you go,
Do not worry,
They won't say no.

If people are being mean to you,
Just ignore,
Because if you don't,
It will just hurt you more.

Never give up,
Always put up a fight,
Because if you don't,
You will not earn your right.

Be strong, be nice, be all that you can,
Because no one can stop you,
Because you're gonna act like a man.

Dillan Maskill (12)
Castleford Academy, Castleford

Why Is It Different?

Why is it different
To love someone the same as everyone else?
Why does it matter so much?
Why do you care?

Why is it different
When someone on the TV happens to be gay?
Why are you shocked?
We are all the same!

Why is it different
When we are masculine?
For you it's normal!
Yet, when I do it, it's faking!
Even when I'm feminine I'm forcing it.
Why won't you leave me alone?

Why is it different?
Does my existence bother you?
Shock you? Scare you?

Please tell me!
How am I different to you?

Harry Johnson (12)
Castleford Academy, Castleford

We Are Like Space

We're like space
We have parts filled with grace,
But people don't see that trace.
Making beauty a race
We are like space.

Like a star.
They make grown people dream
About things they think they 'need'
But that star doesn't shine,
It burns.

A meteor.
It lands after miles of travelling
And makes an unbeautiful landing
But that meteor is a star,
A shooting star.

Space is like us.
It has parts with grace,
We mostly look at that trace,
Winning beauty's race.
We are like space.

Madison Duggan (11)
Castleford Academy, Castleford

Dreams

Sometimes life is tricky
Or things get sticky
Sometimes things go wrong
Or you feel like you don't belong.

Use your voice
It is your choice
Spread the word
It is time to be heard.

Don't run from fear
Be as free as a deer
Perfection is found in imperfection
Follow your dreams
No matter how things seem.

If you don't say
You won't change by the day.

Everything is possible
You are unstoppable
Don't act like you don't exist
When you should tick off your checklist.

Emily Shillito (12)
Castleford Academy, Castleford

My Empowered Poem

You gave me strength, you gave me happiness
You helped me when I was in the dumps
And because of this, I love you.

You gave me joy, you gave me elevation
You comforted me
And because of this, I love you.

You gave me confidence, you gave me encouragement
You always listened to me on a night
And because of this, I love you.

You are my life, you are my treasure
But most of all you're my life
And because of this, I love you.

You are my soul
The person I love
And for this, I love you.

Freddie Moran (11)
Castleford Academy, Castleford

Why Did They Say That?

If you're not a perfect princess
You are not their interest
They don't care what you feel
They will just tell people you steal
If you don't have the best clothes, followers, face or body
They won't treat you like you're somebody
They will put you down just because you have the wrong shoes
They will put you down without any clues
But this is not a reason to cry
All you need to do is take a big fat sigh
You are better and more powerful
They're no better than being sour and dull.

Bethany Dixon (12)
Castleford Academy, Castleford

Our World

Sometimes it rains,
Sometimes it snows,
Sometimes the sun shows,
Sometimes the wind blows.

The climate changes all the time,
Affecting the lives of all of us.
Animals die,
The birds can't fly,
And not many animals survive.

Fire spreads as the world sheds,
Smoke fills the air.
Since people show no care,
The Earth slowly disappears
As everyone starts to fear.

The world is ours
For us to protect,
So why do we kill it instead?

Thomas Graham (12)
Castleford Academy, Castleford

It's Okay

It's okay not to be perfect,
Your beauty is not everything,
Love yourself in every way,
Always keep your crown on.

It's okay to be yourself,
Don't change for someone else,
You are your own beauty,
That's what makes you you!

It's okay to be different,
No matter what's your appearance,
Just keep believing
And keep succeeding.

It's okay to feel love,
Even when life's hard,
Have faith
And it's okay.

Molly Wilby (12)
Castleford Academy, Castleford

All About Me

When I was small I knew nothing at all
But when I grew tall I thought I knew it all.

Sometimes there was laughter and tears
But throughout the years I learned to be able to cheer.

As I grew older I became wise and bolder.
Learning to shine bright without fear or fright.
I am happy in me and that's all I need to be.

I am rich in family and love
That is all I will ever need for me to succeed
Being happy and not sad I learned life isn't too bad.

Evie Smith (12)
Castleford Academy, Castleford

Myself

I want to be brave,
I want to be confident,
I want to be like everybody else,
I want to be everyone but me,
I want to be, wait...
That has to change,
I need to be myself.
I am confident,
I am brave,
I am powerful,
I am...
I'm like thunder,
I'm like a tiger,
I'm like the weather,
I'm like a flower,
I'm like...
Be yourself,
Don't let anyone make you change,
Be yourself,
Be yourself today.

Eva Wilby (12)
Castleford Academy, Castleford

Thank You

Thank you for being there.
Thank you for looking after me.
Thank you for loving me.

When I'm at my lowest you're there.
When you're not here I always find you.
When you're at your lowest I'm always here.

Thank you for always being there.
Thank you for loving me.
When I'm down you're always there.

And I just want to say thank you
For everything you have done.

Summer Devonshire (12)
Castleford Academy, Castleford

Independent

Women.
They get told what to do.
Every one of us, even you.

Do this, do that, and all the rest,
Makes us feel very depressed,
Our body is ours and nobody else's.
When we post online, some of our selfies
The comments make us insecure,
There are very few people that give us support.

We are not toys,
We are human beings just like you,
We are independent
And you can be too.

Kate Wadsworth (11)
Castleford Academy, Castleford

Family

Family is everything you need.
They helped you during the darkest times.
They put food on the table.
They let you have free speech.
They gave you clothes.
They said, "Hey, it's going to be okay."
They stood up for you.

They helped you.
They loved you.
They accepted you with open arms.
And after all that,
You said, "Thank you."

Family is everything.

Will Connell (12)
Castleford Academy, Castleford

Skeletons

Skeletons, oh skeletons
They're all up in our skin.

Skeletons, oh skeletons
They help you do your thing.

Skeletons, oh skeletons
They structure your floppy skin.

Skeletons, oh skeletons
Without them you'd be like jelly-ton.

Skeletons are such strange things,
That we need to live.

If we didn't have them
We wouldn't be able to live.

Lennon Scholey (11)
Castleford Academy, Castleford

We Are Humans

We are humans
And none of us are the same
But that's what makes us cool
So we don't need to change.

Some of us just do our thing
Some of us want to fit in
But we don't need to, you are you
You don't need change, and that is true.

You don't need to feel ashamed
Or think you need to change
Because nobody is the same
And that's why we are humans.

Megan Thorogood (12)
Castleford Academy, Castleford

Only Eight Minutes

Only eight minutes,
Under your knees,
We only had to march,
We only had to stand up for what's right,
It's fine.
Only eight minutes,
We had to fight,
When we shouldn't have to,
For BLM is what I believe in,
For George Floyd, I stand with him,
For the bullets that got shot at the people I trust,
You wouldn't understand,
But for now
I guess it's fine.

Laycee-Mai Cockerham (12)
Castleford Academy, Castleford

How Football Has Helped Me

You gave me life, you gave me hope,
You gave me a place where I belonged.

You gave me life, you gave me hope,
You gave me strength,
You gave me joy,
You gave me laughter and
When things got tough you gave me the safety net to fall.

I had a reason to strive on forwards to the wet grassy field.
You gave me life, you gave me hope,
You gave me a football family.

Olivia Paul (12)
Castleford Academy, Castleford

Don't Call Me That!

I might be fat,
But that don't mean you can call me that.
In fact you shouldn't make anyone feel like that.
Cos that's horrible and you don't just do that.

You may not like them
But that isn't an excuse,
Change yourself,
Don't be like that.

No matter who you are,
Big or small,
You should feel welcome,
No hate anymore.

Alexander Bell (12)
Castleford Academy, Castleford

This Is Me

I believe in me,
That's all I need,
I don't need others to put me down,
I will stand up and talk,
I shall do it for my mates, family, people I love,
Nobody is the same,
Everyone's different,
Being perfect in their own way,
Spots, scars, different skin colour or type,
It doesn't matter,
Because everyone is unique in their own different way.

Ruby Hamer (12)
Castleford Academy, Castleford

You

The words that hurt you
Made you feel like a fool
I wear a uniform and you do too
But always be you.

We all look the same
Which can't raise our fame
Clothing isn't a game
And we all have a different shape
So just be you.

Embrace your flaws
Instead of creating the cause
And even if hatred wounds you like claws
Just be you.

Mariana Whiteley (12)
Castleford Academy, Castleford

Your Body

Your body helps you.
Your eyes help you see.
Your nose helps you smell.
Your mouth lets your voice be heard.

You should love the body you are in because it loves you.
You are limitless.
You can be anything.
You are endless.
Just be you.
We each receive a body that is different and unique
So you should love your body, not somebody else's.

Laura Marshall-Jones (12)
Castleford Academy, Castleford

The Nature

Many people stuck on their phone.
Go out! Go row a boat!
Take a nice walk in the park.
Don't let technology get in the way of the spark.
Enjoy the fresh air and all things nice.
Make the decision, change your life.
Snapchat, TikTok and Twitter.
Forget it, it's all just bitter!
Go out, spend time with your friends,
Put all the devices to an end.

Bree Macdonald (12)
Castleford Academy, Castleford

My Mum

You gave birth to me.
You taught me how to talk.
You taught me how to walk.

You were there when I got hurt
And there to put me to bed.

You were there when I was scared
And you were there when I needed a shoulder to cry on.

You reassured me when I was worried.
You do this because you're my mum.

Corey McNichol (12)
Castleford Academy, Castleford

Veganism

V eganism helps the environment
E at a plant-based diet
G reens are good for you
A nimals deserve to live wild
N o Meat Mondays is a start
I t's an interesting diet
S upporting animals is what you do
M eals are good even without meat

Be vegan!

Juno Whitworth (12)
Castleford Academy, Castleford

What Is Empowerment To Me?

What is empowerment to me?
I understood what it was but only to a certain degree

I had a definition
But no recognition
Of it in myself

I thought of what made me feel confident and brave
Something I did where I stepped out of my little cave

But I couldn't find much, I haven't felt a lot yet
And I realised that I should look at this like a threat
A threat of my happiness, a threat to my wellbeing

I thought about it every night
I tried to write about something bright

I felt like everything was going wrong
I had felt that way for so, so long

I couldn't write of anything but being miserable
I felt like nothing was going well, so it was considerable

But eventually, I found out what to do
I want to share my challenges, to help everyone too

It's when you accept that you are struggling
And remove all the weights and insecurities you've been juggling

And when you understand that things don't have to be perfect
Even if things aren't right, you can get that feeling that feels correct

It's a feeling that makes you shift in your seat
A feeling that makes your chest thud to a quick beat

It's a feeling that no one really knows how to explain
They think it's complicated, something hard to maintain

You might know exactly what you need
You know what you want and just can't succeed

But it is unembellished and bare
Straightforward and right there

You need to notice the build-up of everything that was flawless
You need to romanticise all that was once awe-less

The little things you read about in a book
You realise are happening to you if you merely take a closer look.

You need to realise that everything is great,
That all those bad feelings are only things you create

You need to realise that it's an achievement to get out of bed
To block the thoughts that course through your head

That it's something that should make your face flush with pride
Focus on the little things that you used to just abide

Focus on your hair when it glows autumnally like leaves
Like when they sway softly, sinking from trees

Focus on the smell of the place you visit most
A bookshop full of stories to get entirely engrossed

Focus on your cosy bed, sheets crisp and warm
You nestle in your teddies' folds, relax, adjust and conform

Focus on your dad's nickname for you, the one that makes you laugh
Laughter swarms you so much your sister must speak on your behalf

Focus on the nice tea Mum made for your arrival from school
It's lemony and sweet, it's warm and not too cool

Focus on your teacher's words and the way she says her Rs
The way it purrs and hums, like the engine reels in cars

Focus on the sky when it reaches dusk
Like a painter spilt his paints, all the tones of rust

Focus on the way your best friend says your name
Like you're really loved and they like who you became

Fous on the way some people say 'I love you'
It feels good, especially when it's true

But what happens when you start to feel self-love?
It may sound cheesy, but you feel above...

Above all those people and the things that they post -
The messages and comments that make you feel like a ghost

You feel on top of the world
You dance, and sing, and jump, and twirl

You feel boundless and in control
You're in power, and you've got the main role

So, what is empowerment to me?
Knowing I can pick myself up, that I've got the key
The key to feeling happy
Happy and free.

Leela Nayak (12)
Clapton Girls' Academy, Hackney

Where I Belong

Loud noises,
One topic I try to avoid.
It's hard to though.

Walking into school,
The noises growing with every step I take.
Thumping at my eardrums,
Feeling like tidal waves,
Trying to drown me.

Dazed, I walk to my classes,
Sound filling up the halls.
Chattering and shouting everywhere I turn,
No escape.

I rush to class.
I get a few minutes silence
But then the 'loud ones' enter,
Talking and shoving each other joyfully.
I slowly take deep breaths.

The 'trouble makers' chewing gum loudly,
Talking back to the teacher.
I can't focus.

The 'artsy one' sketching,
Pestering me for stationery,

Shouting out randomly,
I shut my ears.

The teacher tells us off,
Screaming at us,
Orders me to open my ears.
I don't want to.
My teacher pulls my fingers away
And tells me to stand outside.

I walk out with everyone murmuring,
Wondering what was going on.
My teacher follows me outside,
I hear a thunderous rumble of talking straight away.

Ms asks if something's wrong,
I shake my head.
She asks if I'm sure,
I nod.

Not daring to look at Ms, we walk back inside.
The alarm bell rings.
Everyone packs up,
The sounds of pens knocking together,
Bags opening and closing,
Rulers clanging onto the floor,
Papers rustling,
I just want to scream.

I just want to run away.
I just want some quiet.

Last lesson of the day,
A sense of relief rushes through me.
I've just got this lesson and the weekend is here,
One more lesson and I'm finally free.
Just one more hour.

The lesson is almost finished,
It feels like I've just had an audition,
Testing me if I can cope with the noise.

10 minutes...
8 minutes...
3 minutes...

Suddenly, a loud scream echoes through the room.
I jolt out of my seat.
I can't breathe.
Imaginary hands start clamping themselves tightly around my chest.
I reach for my bag,
Clawing at the zip,
Wishing I could be at home,
Wishing people understood,
Wishing I could drown out the noise,
Wishing it wasn't so hard.

I grab my inhaler and puff three times,
I feel better.
The teacher helps me up,
She packs up my things and pats me on the back.

The bell starts ringing.
I run outside,
Not wanting to look back,
Not wanting to return to this hellhole.

Scattered laughter and chaos everywhere I turn.
I feel like a pig, being ripened until slaughter day.

So many noises,
Thumping at my eardrums,
Feeling like tidal waves,
Drowning me.

I want to cry,
I want to lie down and sleep,
And never wake.
I just want to go home.

Stumbling through the streets,
Cars honking at me,
People staring.
But I don't care,
I'm almost home,
I'm almost there.

My mum is waiting for me at the doorstep.
I stagger into her arms,
Sobbing into her chest,
Her warm embrace calming me,
Her hand stroking my head,
Saying everything will be okay,
Her heartbeat loud but soothing.

She takes me upstairs,
And brings me a warm cup of milk,
Sitting next to me,
Understanding.

She takes my empty cup
And wipes away the froth on my mouth,
She leaves me alone,
In the peace and quiet,
Alone with the birds singing,
Alone with the slight sound of light rain,
Alone with nobody but myself.
This is where I belong.

Mei Foo Sherwin (11)
Clapton Girls' Academy, Hackney

Forest

One afternoon I said to myself,
"Why isn't the thick timberland more delicate?"
Down, down, down into the darkness of the thick timberland,
Gently it goes - the difficult, the unsmooth, the rough.

The geographic region that's really parched,
Above all other is the wooded wilderness.
A wooded wilderness is dry, a wooded wilderness is baked,
A wooded wilderness is sun-baked, however.
The woolly, glad greenwood sings like a wild girl
Never forget the soft and muddled glad greenwood.

How happy are zany, wet woods!
Mutter.
Why are they so zany?

I cannot help but stop and look at the industrial, scientific silviculture.
Now blue-collar is just the thing
To get me wondering if the scientific silviculture is highly developed.

The bristled brush is not inhabited!
The bristled brush is exceptionally unoccupied.

Are you upset by how unpeopled it is?
Does it tear you apart to see the bristled brush so unoccupied?

Delicia Ekutsu Mbala (12)
Clapton Girls' Academy, Hackney

A Silent Birdsong

The sun stretched its lazy rays of light
Through the interlocked branches.
Somewhere, in the outstretched equilibrium
A bird sang.
The melody rang
It rang across fields of corn,
Through acres of dark woods,
Under bridges,
It swam with the minnows,
With the ripples in the icy-clear water,
It echoed through cavernous caves,
And then it stopped.

Silence overpowered.
The world turned grey.
Storms raged, and hurricanes came.
Devastation reigned.
Those who wanted to speak had been maimed.
And when it truly mattered, our world had been divided.
With so-called 'right-minded'
Against
Those left 'short-sighted'.
Colour was sucked from every inch of our planet,
Corn stopped growing,
Woods became darker,
The minnows stopped swimming in the icy-clear water.

The cavernous caves became crowded,
Those who were lost had started hiding.
Hiding from society, hiding from each other,
Hiding from their sisters, hiding from their brothers
Until a day came,
When one had decided
That they'd had enough of being divided;
'Right-minded' v 'short-sighted'.
They had found their rainbow,
A rainbow of hope,
A rainbow of knowing who they were was enough,
A rainbow of knowing to never give up.
So they carried that rainbow, in their heart forever
And braved the dangers through the cold, stormy weather.
They knew who they were,
And that was enough.
They could do anything.
They were so tough.

They stood up for themselves, though they were knocked down,
And soon the grey had slowly turned to brown.
They kept pushing their boulder up their hill,
Like Sisyphus did, like he does still.
They carried on and on,
Until the day, when others decided
That they'd had enough of being divided;
'Right-minded' v 'short-sighted'

And the caves became cavernous instead of crowded,
The minnows went swimming in icy-cold water,
The woods became bright,
And the corn grew.

And a bird sang a song,
With a slightly different tune.

Scarlett Quinn (13)
Clapton Girls' Academy, Hackney

Anger

I saw the uncontrollable suffering of my generation destroyed,
How I mourned the anguish,
Down, down, down into the darkness of the anguish,
Gently it goes - the irrepressible, the incorrigible, the unmanageable.

One afternoon I said to myself,
Why isn't the angst more conservative?
Down, down, down, into the darkness of the angst,
Gently it goes - the progressive, the inexact.

How happy is the woolly unease!
Does the unease make you shiver?
Does it?

The emotional state that's really zany,
Above all others is the unhappiness,
Does the unhappiness make you shiver?
Does it?

I cannot help but stop and look at the fierce hostility,
Never forget the merciless and intense hostility.

The nauseate that's really teenage,
Above all others is the outrage,
Now young is just the thing,
To get me wondering if the outrage is immature.

Yasmin Ali (12)
Clapton Girls' Academy, Hackney

I Am...

I am brave
I am bold
I am strong
Power is what I hold
I always, *always* know what to do
What turn to take
What;
Left or
Right or
Up or
Down
Never do I take the incorrect;
Left or
Right or
Up or
Down
I am always correct
For the power of knowledge, that is my head.

The strength I have?
It's something new
And would never belong to someone like you.
That book of knowledge,
So fierce
So bold, so mighty and great -
So engraved

So empowered
Empowered
That strength is as reckless as the lions and boars
That are established in the wild
That hunt down their prey
That stay on their guard throughout the *whole* day
Like a jewel
So phosphorescent
So blazing
Brighter than the rays the sun exchange
I am blessed with this knowledge
So pure
So true
Being empowered
It's what I must be to you.

Though, at my lowest, of lows
That isn't me.
that isn't me
I'm clumsy
I'm silly
I'm reckless
I'm childish
I *always* take the incorrect right
It gets me into trouble
I don't want trouble
I do not want to get into trouble
I am not real

I am fake
I put on a face
For those who stand in the prejudiced place
I act
And act
And close myself up
Like dry ice in a plastic bottle
I will explode.

One day
Or night
Or evening
Or honeymoon
And that great book of knowledge
That hovers on my head
Will fall and rip apart
And I will go from
Being who I am
To being who I am
But of course, I must continue to put on my act
And I will continue to be great and empowered
For it is what I *must* be to you
But
What am I?

Adesewa Agunlejika (13)
Clapton Girls' Academy, Hackney

Up And Down

Roller coaster, fast, emotional, exciting
That love. Daddy's daughter
Sweet, innocent, hopeful, naive
Absent you were yet all I did was follow
The track was long, I was hopeful
Unlike you I'm not anymore.

Infant to adolescence is where it took place
Detachment, realisation, anger
Over and over and over again those three words
I miss you, I'll come back, I love you
But all that was paramount to me suddenly became insignificant with your absence
We're approaching another rise on this ride
Yet again I wonder...
How are you right next to me but not at all?

Finally taking the lead on this ride has come to an end for me
But for you it carries on, sweet, innocent, hopeful, naive
I walk away from the track, cynical, adult
I look back, watching you read him aimlessly
It's still you, unchanged
Hope is no more as our bond remains unfinished and partial.

Temitayo Fayehun (16)
Clapton Girls' Academy, Hackney

I Keep Them At Heart

I present to you the three rules I keep at heart to flourish.
I strive not to wish, for if I wish
I shall inevitably miss.
The world though not full of bliss,
Is why I aspire to convince,
That you should work for a cause,
Not for applause.
It may be hard,
But does that mean you should discard?
No, because no matter how hard,
You should play the cards you have been given in your yard,
Once you have played your cards,
You will have a guard.
And there barred
Is what would've been you scarred.
Scarred at a distance.
While you stride through a gorgeous boulevard.
Now remember, the beings that respect you.
The one who left angry and bitter comes back,
The one who left smiling doesn't.
Now don't ask why,
You know why,
because caring for them,
You didn't try.
So much, they reciprocated your actions with a goodbye.

Look at you now, notified with a bye and disqualified.
See, that doesn't need to be you,
So as long as you keep your world away from the colour blue,
Keep it bright
And don't say it's fate, because you have been given free will,
The words you said were not through fate,
But the result of what you yourself had propagate.
To keep your world bright, ask yourself,
Is it right, is it just?
Was it a mere plight,
And is it a must?

Ifeoluwa Adams (14)
Clapton Girls' Academy, Hackney

Scars

Scars can mean different things to different people
They can remind you of something good or something bad
They could remind you of something joyful or maybe even something evil.

Everyone has a scar or two or maybe even three
Some are visible while others are not
But all types of scars still mean the same to me.

Scars that people can see make others feel low
So learn to love your scars
Because that will help you to grow.

Scars are evidence of where you've been
And shows you where you're going
But it also shows your journey and what you've seen.

A scar is a power in itself
It shows that you've been hurt but you have healed
So learn to love your scars to love oneself.

The scars you can't see are the hardest to heal
Those are the scars that make *you* you
But those are the scars that tell you how you feel.

If a person sees a scar they think bad things
People should be encouraging you to love your scars
But every time someone has that same reaction it really stings.

Wear your scars like they are wings
They can become a huge part of your life
So learn to love your scars for new beginnings.

Aya Ramdane (13)
Clapton Girls' Academy, Hackney

The Struggle Of Choice

We are all supposed to choose
But what if we can't?
They say we cannot lose
But what if we can?
I know I have many years ahead
To choose my own future
But the choice is so hard I might rather be dead
When I sit alone next to the towering trees
I can always see them dance
To the soothing sound of the wind
But they have no choice
It's easier that way
And the clouds in the sky
Circle the Earth several times
They have a race around the Earth
To see who's the fastest cloud.
They're as white as snow
But as shallow as glass
They watch every city
As the pollution grows
But they can't do anything
As they don't have a voice
But it's easier that way
Now I have a choice
I make many every day

If it was all the same I would never
Need to choose but without a voice
I would never be heard
I don't know, the choice is too hard!

Halima Ayub (11)
Clapton Girls' Academy, Hackney

All Our Fault

It's all your fault
It's all our fault
Our world is screeching
Crying
Yelling
Salty tears racing down its cheeks
Falling down on its knees and begging for us to stop
To stop multiplying
To stop our extinction

Whilst we are living
Everything is draining
And soon we're going to be brought down with them
it's inevitable
Like a balloon about to pop
Like daisies plucked from the ground
We're running out of time
And it's our fault
It's all our fault

Can't you see what we've done?
What we've created?
What we're doing?

It's not too late though
It's never too late
If we act now we could stop our extinction

Along with every other creature we live with on this planet
This beloved planet.

All I'm asking you
is one question
It's very simple

Do you feel guilty?

Lydia Bilen-Alonso (12)
Clapton Girls' Academy, Hackney

Claustrophobia

Claustrophobia
The fear of small spaces, being trapped.
But how does it feel to be trapped in your own body?
To never feel wrong, but never feel right?
To never feel free, but never feel tight?
To want nothing more than to go off and take flight?
Claustrophobia
You're scared of being stuck, you can't move.
But how does it feel to be stuck in your own head?
The voices in your brain like hissing vipers telling you to change.
The anxious thump-thump of your heart telling you to stay the same.
And the quiet whispering of your soul telling you it doesn't know the way.
Claustrophobia
A fear that, like any, you can overcome.
You can overcome this.
Not a woman, but proud.
Not a man, but proud.
Nothing like anything you've seen before
And so, so proud.
Break free from these chains because you're proud.

Maya Schwartz (12)
Clapton Girls' Academy, Hackney

It's Not Fair

Normal - I thought it was normal at least,
Pull your skirt down, young lady,
That top's too open, cover up,
It stings but you stuff it in,
And it hurts every woman within,
It's not fair.

You look overweight,
You're so bony, what happened?
A sea storm brumes in your eyes,
As your body cries,
You check a scale,
As your eyes suck up the piercing sorrow wails,
It's not fair.

For every woman in our city,
For every woman in our country,
For every woman in the world,
They don't need your opinion,
They don't want it,
Not one bit,
They weren't made in a factory
And neither were you,
So if I was you
I would stop too
Because it isn't fair.

Sophia Westwood (12)
Clapton Girls' Academy, Hackney

I Love You

I love you
You never fail
To make me smile
You never fail
To make me happy
And that
Is why I love you.

I love you
You never fail
To make me laugh
You never fail
To be affectionate
And that
Is why I love you.

I love you
You never fail
To be honest
You never fail
To be loving
And that
Is why I love you.

I love you
You never fail
To be cheerful

You never fail
To be okay
And that
Is the only thing
I don't love about you.

You don't have to be okay
You don't have to be perfect
You have to let go
To feel free.

You aren't expected
To be okay
You aren't expected
To be joyful.

Just please
For me
Be yourself.

I love you.

Anouk Lawless-Monnot (12)
Clapton Girls' Academy, Hackney

Why Don't You Care?

It really is true that no one is too young to make a difference,
But you still don't turn your head.
Why don't you care or is it just that you are uneducated?
If you don't make a difference,
This is not just a little interference.
Your kids' great-grandkids' world could disappear in the blink of an eye.
Now don't tell me I am being drastic,
Don't tell me that I am telling a lie.
This pollution and this littering, why do you say this is all a myth?
All this proof, you say it is all these activists just goofing around.
Now I will ask again, now answer with the truth...
Why don't you care?

Margot Staves (11)
Clapton Girls' Academy, Hackney

Slow Summer

Winter, summer, spring, fall,
I want to have it all
But I have to wait as long as it will take.
Summer is far but I won't get there by car
I hope it comes fast, fast as it can go.
I miss summer,
The warmth on me
Or on my hand which is holding the key.
Slow summer, is it slow?
By the time I get there I will be old
And then it will go back to cold.
Slow summer,
Why when I am around, why me?
Slow summer,
I want to be free
But I will wait as long as it will take.
I hope I don't break before summer takes.
Slow summer
I will wait 100 years to see it in full shine again.

Mia Breen (13)
Clapton Girls' Academy, Hackney

Our Earth

Orangutans swinging to the beat of the trees,
Sweeping the grass as they sway in the breeze,
Air as crisp as the shot of a gun,
All the plants reaching their hands to the sun.

Under a grand willow tree's hue,
With leaves that droop from the weight of the dew I lie...

To you.
I'm actually sitting amongst sad ashes,
Of something, that was beautiful beyond comprehension.

It became the fuel of human greed,
The green paper they need,
Tree by tree,
Forest by forest,
Casting dark shadows and bruises over the land of our birth,
Our Earth.

Ella-May Smith (13)
Clapton Girls' Academy, Hackney

This Generation

This generation cries
Father God.
The evil, the hatred,
The violence and death swallow this generation
Father God.
Lockdown, a search for help,
For a friend,
For guidance and for peace.
BLM!
We chanted yet no change has been made,
We are given free will
Yet we decide to hate, discriminate, hurt,
Destroy and kill each other.
'Love thy neighbour',
Is there any love left in this generation
Father God?
I sit back and wonder,
Where has all the love gone?
This generation cries
And I know only you can help us
Father God.

Gabriella Arthur (14)
Clapton Girls' Academy, Hackney

Kashmir Be Free

Run, run!
As they hear the sound of the shot of the gun.

Cries, cries!
Of the children falling in eternal sleep in the dead of the night.

Why, why?
They wonder as the screams echo through the twilight sky.

Do you remember, remember,
When the valley was full of laughter and joy?

Remember, remember,
When the chakor spread its wings with freedom in its eyes,

Oh I pray, I pray,
I pray that Kashmir will be free someday,

So please, please, Kashmir be free.

Qurratulain Muhammad (12)
Clapton Girls' Academy, Hackney

Standards

Standards...
I hate them, yet, I have no choice but to fit the rest,
If I fit the beauty standard, I'm trying too hard.
If I dress like a guy, I don't take care of myself.
Why?
Why do I have to please everyone?
Why can't I be proud of myself?
Why can't I be myself without being judged?
Well, that's just it...
I can't and I never can
So my feelings and personality
Will remain hidden behind this mask
For as long as I stay in this toxic place: School.

Judea-Amalla James (13)
Clapton Girls' Academy, Hackney

School

As my alarm goes off for school
I wake up and regain my fuel
I get dressed and look at the time
When I realised it was half-nine
I left in a rush
Whilst putting on blush
And I fell in a pool
Whilst running to school
I got up soaked
And I full-on choked
I never made it on time
Which was considered a crime
I was met by a teacher
Who looked like a creature
She told me I got a detention
And if I didn't go it would end up in a suspension.

Amarah Navsa (13)
Clapton Girls' Academy, Hackney

Power

I've always aspired to be a leader,
A powerful woman to right the wrongs,
To empower and inspire others,
To give compassion, advice and comfort,
For ones who may seek help.

I've always aspired to be powerful,
To show people it's okay to be different,
To lead people to a right path,
To show them the wonders of life,
To let them know that life is precious,
To cherish the little things.

Shayane Khan (14)
Clapton Girls' Academy, Hackney

Living Like Me

Sometimes it's hard
Living in their shadow
Sometimes it's hard
Being so shallow
But underneath all the fun and games
There's someone sad
Someone in pain.

Living like me is not the best
It's often hard and makes me stressed
But when it's hard
And when I struggle
I try to remember
It's worth the trouble.

Addison Woods (12)
Clapton Girls' Academy, Hackney

Haiku Poetry

Icy mountaintops
Wind breezing through mellow lungs
A breath of fresh air.

Chilly sunrise stroll
Frost-covered cherry blossoms
Surviving the cold.

Under splitting ice
Shivering fractals forming
Like splattering glass.

Aasiya Salahuddin Khan (12)
Clapton Girls' Academy, Hackney

A Fluffy Friend

Cats are cute, adorable and company for when you're feeling down.
Bundles of fluff and happiness to look forward to after school.
They're also quite independent so they won't stress you out.
Clean out their litter trays, feed them, love them and that's pretty much it.
But indoor or outdoor depends on quite a lot.
If you have a scaredy-cat, and it doesn't like going out
You will have to play with it yourself.
This will be useful if you want to do exercise as well
Because they don't bring the toy back to you.
Outdoor cats will have their own fun,
But make sure to greet them with a bath when they come home,
Because they will definitely be dirty.
Now, I don't know whether or not you've tried it before
But bathing a cat isn't easy.
There will not be a day when you've finished bathing a cat with bare hands and haven't got a single scratch on them.
It's a challenge, and also, be prepared to get wet,
Because they'll always jump out and spread water everywhere.
Now, what do you do after a bath?
You snuggle up into bed, right?
Well make sure to make space for your cat and for yourself.

You're probably thinking, what's my point?
I'll tell you what... Go and get a bundle of fluff
And it'll turn your whole life another way round.

Faizah Ali (14)
Dixons McMillan Academy, Bradford

The Four Seasons

Spring
A bunny softly hops its gentle stop,
Blossom trees are all around,
Soon we'll begin our Easter prep,
We can hear chicks chirping, what a beautiful sound.

Summer
The sun is out now we know summer is here,
Time to get your tennis rackets out, it's time for summer sports,
We are on the cobbled street playing with our friends, what can we hear?
It's the ice cream truck, parked on the tennis court.

Autumn
Whilst walking on the path colourful leaves are falling on me,
At school my favourite thing to do is to collect conkers,
Acorns is all I see,
All this incredible nature is making me go a bit bonkers.

Winter
I'm so thrilled for Christmas Day,
Time to get the decorations up,
Snow is all around so let's play,
Now it's time for a scrumptious hot chocolate cup.

Eliza Hussain (12)
Dixons McMillan Academy, Bradford

Martin Luther King

Martin Luther King, he had the greatest dream.
It could only be a thing if they worked as a team.
Something was very wrong, he had to be strong.
He had to work at a quick pace,
Judged by the colour of his race.
He gave the greatest speech, for everyone to preach.
Wanted his kids to survive, his words remain today alive.
His pictures black and white, he had to hold on tight.
Slaved by his skin, he had to fight and win.
He was not a real king, he hadn't horses, a crown or anything.
He really had to suffer and his skin he had to cover.
Then he was murdered by those who denied,
The news spread quickly worldwide.
Those who killed him, wanted for arrest,
As he was shot in the chest.
He died only at 39, everyone remained on his line.
Martin Luther King had the greatest dream,
It could be a thing if they worked as a team.

Shahmeer Nousherwan (13)
Dixons McMillan Academy, Bradford

Covid

We were unfortunate to have a pandemic.
It was so scary.
All we could do was pray.

All over the world people were dying.
Mothers, fathers, daughters were crying.
We were in a horrible situation.
Thank the Lord, we finally found a vaccination.

The prime minister announced a lockdown
We weren't allowed to visit our relatives' houses,
Never mind going into town.
It was so sad losing someone and not being able to say goodbye.
Everywhere cases were exceptionally high.

Then I heard some news, which I couldn't believe.
The prime minister was having a party!
He got caught red-handed
With his bushy, fluffy hair,
He realised what he did, which was really unfair.

Then he said, "Everything will be back to normal!"
What a relief!

Amina Wasim (12)
Dixons McMillan Academy, Bradford

I'll Always Remember

Wherever I go
I feel so low
Since you're not here
I feel like you made a part of me disappear
I remember your smile
Even if it lasted only for a while
I remember how you'd glow
Whilst watching your favourite shows
The way you'd get mad
If anyone made me sad
I remember that night
Your final night
Now you're dead
And I can't get it out of my head
I wanted to be by your side
On this scary ride
But then came the end
And we lost our best friend
But I'm happy you're not in pain
I remember on your funeral it didn't rain
Instead the sun was shining bright
Because you are now part of its light.

Malaika Rafiq (12)
Dixons McMillan Academy, Bradford

Thank You, Dad

You gave me strength, I battled my fear
That's because I knew you were always here
You gave me hope, you gave me shelter
Thank you, I feel better.

I'm grateful I'm here
I live because of you
You are astonishing
We will always know that's true.

You fed me, protected me and cared for me
I will follow that
You taught me, guided me and entertained me
I will cherish that.

You are my leader
You're also my teacher
So I will not fear
Because you're always here.

Saif Farooq (12)
Dixons McMillan Academy, Bradford

Rights

Rights are important for everyone
Because they represent who we are
But if we don't respect everyone's rights we won't get far
Rights are what we stand for
It helps us to encourage more
But if we don't respect our rights more
It will make our heads sore
Rights clearly show who stands for what
Disrespect you they should not
You have got to fight for your rights
Otherwise nothing seems right
Everyone should be treated fairly
Unfortunately we see that rarely.

Mohammed Naeem (12)
Dixons McMillan Academy, Bradford

Summer

If summer was a person,
She would be a little girl at the beach in flip-flops.
Summer would wear nothing that makes them warm
But rather things that make them feel alive.
Summer would smell like a vibrant freshness,
A juicy sweetness,
Nothing but heaven.
Summer would spend the day in peace,
Resting, locked away from the negative thoughts that may invade their mind.
Summer would spend the night not surrounded or drowned in their own ideas,
But in tranquillity and calmness.

Inaaya Lehan (11)
Dixons McMillan Academy, Bradford

I Am So Grateful

You gave me light when I was alone in the dark,
You gave me hope when I was hopeless
And I am so grateful.

You helped me escape the sadness when I was upset,
You helped me escape the pain when I was hurt
And I am so grateful.

You healed me when I was hurt,
You empowered me when I was weak
And I am so grateful.

You shine my sun when the moon comes out,
And I am so grateful,
Thank you, Mother and Sister.

Tyler Khan (11)
Dixons McMillan Academy, Bradford

The Endless Battles

I am but a lost soul
Fighting endlessly to and fro
Living in an infinite light
But I try with all my might
Trying to believe it'll be alright
I am but a pawn in their sight
Tirelessly battling till the night
But I still try to fight
Trying to believe it'll be alright.

I am but a poor soul
Trembling down to the last bone
Hanging on for dear life
Trying to believe it'll be alright.

Abdullah Hussain (13)
Dixons McMillan Academy, Bradford

You Are Unique

Don't ever let anyone overpower you
Don't let it affect what you do
Never look at the negative things about yourself
Look at the positive
Your insecurities are what make you unique
Stand up for yourself
Let your voice be heard
Stand tall and proud
Don't let anyone put you down
Your life, you choose
Don't change for anyone
Your amazing differences are what make you...
Unique.

Daniyah Kamran (12)
Dixons McMillan Academy, Bradford

Spring To Summer

The transitions go from spring to summer
And start to let out beautiful colours.
As the days grow longer and longer
So do the trees
And as the sky gets brighter
You struggle to see.

At night you struggle to sleep
So you wake up and start reading your book,
You start to get lost,
With all the words flying through you,
You start to doze off
And so you sleep with my book on your head.

Fatimah Alzubaedi (11)
Dixons McMillan Academy, Bradford

Empowered

My life is great
It went so straight
I had no problem
But it all went wrong.

It felt like hell
So it wasn't well
It's like I was dead
But not yet.

I had to fight
And do what was right
Not give up on me
And to show
Who I wanted to be.

Now my life is okay
And now I'm awake
Seeing my future
And my brain working
Like a computer.

Anas Hussain (13)
Dixons McMillan Academy, Bradford

My Voice

It's a big world out there
But out of all these voices are people
I may not be the tallest or biggest in the world
Mine may be the smallest
I may not be strong like the tiger
I may not be smart as the leopard
Or fast as the cheetah
Nor as confident as the lion
But I can touch the stars if I stand on my toes
And I know my words will change the world
So you better listen close.

Abeer Haider (11)
Dixons McMillan Academy, Bradford

Limit Breaker

Don't let them hold you back
Put more focus on your studies
And you will bite back
And those people who said you couldn't do it
Show them you can break your limit
Then you will be at the top
And they will be at the bottom asking for a job
Then you'll say,
"Do you remember when you bullied me?"
But now I broke my limit.

Qasim Zaman (13)
Dixons McMillan Academy, Bradford

Love Everyone

We as humans are built in a certain way,
To see the world in a distinct way,
But why has this meant that in a world of such beauty
We separate people from that just cause of genetics?
We should all be together,
To make the world last for generations to come,
To love everyone in such a way
That no other generation has.

Krish Patel (12)
Dixons McMillan Academy, Bradford

Education

Day after day, there's something new that we learn,
From youngsters to elders education is the key.
This shall stay with you forever,
From Shakespeare to brand-new writers,
Education has helped them succeed.
Education is a gift.
Education is the determination,
We should treasure such information.

Ayaan Maroof (12)
Dixons McMillan Academy, Bradford

Summer

Today we will celebrate the start of summer
By taking the sunshine inside.
You will need a full-beam smile,
A heart full of hope,
Lots of friends to come to play awhile,
Puzzles and Lego, a laugh and a joke,
Oreos and ice cream,
Empowered in play,
Giggling together,
It's sunny today!

Ayaan Siddique (12)
Dixons McMillan Academy, Bradford

The War

The war affected all people
The rich and poor people
The nice and mean people

Planes fought in the day
And the war started in May
And has not ended to this day

The soldiers have fought bravely
And they have fought courageously
To protect their country
And the people in it.

Aahyl Alchtar (12)
Dixons McMillan Academy, Bradford

Race To Win

School will take me far
I will be a star
And drive a fast car.

If it all goes to plan
I'll have lots of fans
And have a steering wheel in my hands.

I'll race to win
After school I'll begin
To not follow my dream will be a sin.

Yusuf Satti (12)
Dixons McMillan Academy, Bradford

Nature

Everything is nature,
God gave us this feature.
Birds fly in the sky,
With the clouds passing by.
Animals, humans walk on land,
With the trees giving them a hand.
Everything is working because of you, Nature,
Thank you, God, for giving us this feature.

Shaunak Surve (13)
Dixons McMillan Academy, Bradford

Empowered

You are brave
You are true
And you gave me a hand
When I needed you.

You are loyal
And appear to me as royal
As I always relied on you.

You are affectionate and funny
And for that I am lucky
To have you as my buddy.

Aliza Abid (12)
Dixons McMillan Academy, Bradford

Thank You

I looked at the moon as I sat in my room
My thoughts were as dark as the night's sky
But when I looked at the stars I thought of you
When all was dark you shone in the night sky
This is my way of saying thanks to you.

Aariz Sultan (13)
Dixons McMillan Academy, Bradford

Humanity And Me

Humanity angers me, from the time the first war was fought to the time the first slave was bought.
Humanity causes destruction and begins wars, ruins lives and strips away all hope.
Humanity divides itself into black and white and is built on deceit, murder and greed.
Humanity turned us into a ticking time bomb and transformed a once beautiful green world to a floating piece of rock infested with humans.
Humanity's leaders are the worst of them all as kings, queens, presidents and prime ministers have all the power in the world but do nothing at all.
Global warming, climate change, homelessness, knife crime, wars... all because of humanity.

Yes. Humanity has its many downs but also its ups.
Slaves were freed, Nelson Mandela, MLK and many others challenged the views of the world.
Freedom of speech, BLM, electric cars and charity are all ways to make our world a better place.
Every day when I wake up I think, *what can I do to change this?*
So, yes, humanity angers me but it also empowers me.

Naa Ayorkor (14)
Riverside Secondary School, Barking

Religion Is Power

Religion is everything and can never ever hold you back,
If someone dares to abuse it don't be afraid to attack.
Religion makes you stronger and will always be my friend,
I'll be proud of my religion all the way until the end.

Religion makes me happy, I'll pray every season,
No one can end my belief, not even one reason.
I'll be happy with myself and my God all the way,
No one can ever end my religion, not a chance, never a day.

Religion defines me, and will always remain in my feelings.
Religion makes me proud, and is my source of healing.
I'll will my religion until the day I die,
Until then, religion will always be seen clear from my two eyes.

Farooq Shittu (12)
Riverside Secondary School, Barking

Thinking

I just want to stop.
Stop thinking.
Stop thinking of every move I make.
Why did I say that?
Did anyone notice?
Just let me be.
Okay!

Just stop thinking
And worrying how I look.
Is my hair messy?
Do I look good?

I want to relax,
Stay calm and at peace,
Yet I can't stop thinking
And it makes me so weak.

When I'm alone all things go away,
No thinking of being judged
Or if everything's going to be okay.

I'm happy,
I'm sad,
I'm at home,
I'm glad.

No thinking,
No worrying,
I am finally at peace.

Oriana Solovjova (14)
Riverside Secondary School, Barking

Us In You

Black, black, black, black
They say black don't crack
Guess that's why they opened us up
Whipped us, kicked us, beat us.

They say they love us
Love our hair, our clothes
Our food, our vibes, our love
But they don't really even love us.

They love what they could be
If they were us
They love our hair, our clothes
Our food, our vibes, our love
When it's on them.

Black, black, black, black
They say black don't crack
Guess that's why they wanna be us
Be seen with us, change us, erase us.

Naliim Al-Doegah
Riverside Secondary School, Barking

Home

Long gone from home,
So numb I could turn to stone.
Lost my voice and lost my roots,
A language beautiful like the song of flute.

I miss the springs and fields of white heaven,
The smell of rain from when I was seven.
The taste of my grandmother's food,
That never failed to lift my mood.
The crush of crimson leaves beneath my boots.

I miss home.

For so long I tried to forget,
Who I was and where I came from.
But now I have nothing but respect,
And pride for where I'm from.

And I miss home.

Alexandra Ioana Sava (14)
Riverside Secondary School, Barking

Pets

Mehhh!
Oh the great goats that make me happy
I don't have one, it makes me feel crabby
I love the great horns and fur
This makes me want to purr.

Now onto the next pet I wish to own
A super cat that wants to roam
Cats are just really calm
It's like living in paradise next to a palm.

Ribbit! Ribbit!
Other pets I want are frogs
Also, I really hate dogs
Frogs are really cool
If you disagree you're just a fool.

Siaan Hussain
Riverside Secondary School, Barking

It's Important To Pray

I go to sleep late at night
I have too much on my mind
I can't stay on track.
I never do.

I wake up early every morning
Nothing to do
But I did not have time to pray
I just can't stay on track.

My family prays as well.
Sometimes,
Not all the time.

Another day is over
But I didn't have time to pray
I don't think everyone prays
They should
It heals you.

Briana Reid (13)
Riverside Secondary School, Barking

Football Is Normal

Being a keeper is normal
Being a girl is normal
But the two things together lead to a frown on some
They think to themselves, *no, not football, get away,*
Football is for boys, pretty dresses are for girls.
And I think to myself, *wake up, wake up!*

Winning the league is normal
However to people what isn't real
Is that the whole team is of girls
I think to myself, *wake up, wake up!*

People's opinions are normal
People's judgements are normal
It's okay to think that I am a girl
And I should wear a dress
And have my hair pinned in curls
It's alright to have doubts
But to say out loud...
Think to yourself, *wake up, wake up!*

So when you open your mouth to say,
"No little girls, get off that pitch, get away!"
Just think that this is what they chose
So think to yourself, *wake up, wake up!*
And take a look around,

Have a look at all of the crowd
And realise things aren't always how you see them.

So if someone judges you because you're a girl,
Tell them, "Wake up, wake up!"

Ava Stringer (12)
The Ferrers School, Higham Ferrers

Come On You Titans

Dear Titans,
We train for the game,
We feel the pain,
We score and cheer,
We concede and groan,
At the ref, we have a moan,
But we keep on going.

Dear defence,
Like a concrete wall,
No one gets through,
Tackling hard and putting your body on the line,
You defend as if we're 1-0 up with seven minutes to go,
Even if we're 7-0 down.

Dear midfield,
Up and down the pitch you go,
Never stopping,
Never slowing,
With the pace of a cheetah
And a desire to win like no other,
You don't stop running.

Dear attack,
You shoot,
You score,
Goals galore,

You attack that ball with the ferocity of a tiger,
And you don't stop until that ball nestles in the net.

Dear Titans,
The season has passed,
And we've played our part,
We've had our ups,
And we've had our downs,
And now there's just one thing left to say...
C O Y T!

Liam McConnell (12)
The Ferrers School, Higham Ferrers

Football

There is one thing that would make me smile
I've been waiting for a while
I want to play football all day long
If I'm not my whole life would be wrong.

If I could have anything
It would be a contract
I don't care how much money I make
It's the football I want to take.

If I could have anything
It would be to play for a professional team
I don't care which one
As long as I accomplish my dream.

If I could have anything
It would be football all the way
It's what I love and what I care about
Every moment wondering, *could this be the day?*

There is nothing I want more
Than to be noticed by a scout and they would think
If I don't scout this player I should quit my job,
So hopefully one day I'll be stepping out on a stadium pitch.

It's not about the money
It's not about the glory

I don't want that, I want...
Football to be my life story.

Bradley Cain (12)
The Ferrers School, Higham Ferrers

Encouragement

To my family,
I want to thank you,
For raising me since I was a child
And always being there for me,
So thank you.

To my pets,
I want to thank you
For always being there for me
Even though some of you have passed,
So thank you.

To my school and friends,
I want to say thank you,
For helping me and supporting me
From reception to now,
So thank you.

To my liking of reading,
I want to say thank you
For showing me new worlds
And for helping me to do better at school,
So thank you.

To my liking of films,
I want to say thank you
For showing me new possibilities and amusing me

And for always being there for me to watch,
So thank you.

To my like of science,
I want to say thank you
For educating me on what is possible
And giving me something to be interested in,
So thank you.

Jacob Martin (13)
The Ferrers School, Higham Ferrers

The Lost, Dying Souls

Inside the bustling city walls,
Factories spur on the lost, dying souls,
Darkness erupts from the molten chambers,
Clinging to the fleeting breeze, brandishing sabres,
Choking, strangling, silencing,
The darkness' grip forever tightening.

Floating on top of the uncharted abyss,
Another lost, dying soul that will not be missed,
A shard of glass, shattered and aghast,
As the temperature rises, the hot flush descends,
The shame that it cannot defend.

Hiding inside the prison of home,
Warnings cannot run as fast as they roam,
Searching, seeking, hunting for the lost, dying souls,
To take and engage, to hold all the controls,
Locked in another prison, far from home,
Far from all, all that is known.

The end of time has arrived,
Not much longer until the Earth cannot ever be revived.

Rowan White (13)
The Ferrers School, Higham Ferrers

The Fight For Ukraine

A war to end the world
A country in fright, in a ball all curled
A man that ruins night and day
But to these people he will never stay away.

Oh Mr Putin, all we ask of you
Is to think about what this could do
All he wants is for us not to meddle
While he puts this country in a state of peril.

A night as cold as his heart
The destruction might just happen to start
When the clock strikes four
A sight to be saw
But may no one ever again.

One man may only want peace
While the other wants the world to cease
A man of laughter, song and dance
May just be taking his final prance.

And when all is over, the fight is done
Will this country be left a crumb?
One evil country towering over like a crane
But when worst comes to worst I will fight for Ukraine.

Lucas Denny (12)
The Ferrers School, Higham Ferrers

You Are Enough

Why can't I just be enough?
Why do I have to be a bluff?
We ask these questions every day
Why won't the pain just go away?

What about my happy ending?
I shouldn't have to blend in
I tried to fit in
But being a fake just isn't it.

Dear future me
I hope you understand
You shouldn't hide under a hood
Your insecurities are beautiful
But most of all, you're worth it.

Dear future me
Your importance is key
So is a cup of tea
But most of all
Don't trip and fall
Over other people's jealousy.

So put on a brew
Stir the stew
But most of all
Know you're beautiful.

Be you, be powerful
Be proud, be loud
Be happy, stay happy.

Enjoy yourself
Because you're enough.

Lola Johnson (12)
The Ferrers School, Higham Ferrers

Thank You

They told me I couldn't,
They told me I shouldn't,
They told me I wouldn't,
They would always tell me no,
I would always prove them wrong.

I almost gave up,
They put me down,
I couldn't get back up.

I told my friends,
They are always there to save me,
They told me, "If you believe, you can achieve."
These wise words always stay with me,
At the bottom of my heart.

Now look at me,
My younger self would be proud,
And how much I have overcome,
I always knew my friends would help,
They are always there for me,
I will always be there for them.

Dear future self,
Never give up,
If you are stuck you are not alone,

Your friends will always be there for you,
No matter what.

Keeley Glenn (13)
The Ferrers School, Higham Ferrers

Passion, Desire, Glory

Ay the game, fame and pain,
Promotion, relegation in your grasp.
Cheers all with beers!
Cheers, cheers echo round, all in bound,
The trophy, the trophy, every team's dream,
Ay the game, fame and pain.

Ay the game, fame and pain,
Plans made, friends aid,
Home or away, we always follow.
Everybody on the edge of their seat,
All wondering, *will we be beat?*
The game, everyone's safe spot,
Everyone's highlight of the week.
Ay the game, fame and pain.

Ay the game, fame and pain,
Fans of all ages,
Unite and fight for their point,
The atmosphere all with beer,
People fear as the final whistle comes near and near,
Ay the game, fame and pain.

I will always love you,
The game that brings fame and pain!

Alfie Beynon (13)
The Ferrers School, Higham Ferrers

I Stand Vegan

In a world of science and technology,
Where every human being can be free,
Why do we still rip apart
And devour the flesh of an animal's heart?

And those who fight against this injustice,
Are faced with great prejudice,
Like a defenceless child backed into a corner,
What's wrong with eating flora?

Why can we not be left alone?
We are all the same, skin and bone,
Think of all the parents, sick and worried,
Their kid can't go to school, they'll just get bullied.

But gradually, the world is changing,
Our army grows, the tables are turning,
We look into a future of ethnicity,
A world not burdened by the grasps of inequality.

Sebastian Davies (12)
The Ferrers School, Higham Ferrers

A Sister's Love

Dear Sister
My love for you is like a mother's
You're always there
You've never left my side
And for that I love you.

Dear Sister
You've never failed to make me laugh
Your smile, the most beautiful of all
You never gave up on me
And for that I love you.

Dear Sister
You've lifted my spirits
You fill me with joy and courage
You made me who I am
And for that I love you.

Dear Sister
You filled me with confidence
You loved me more than anyone did
The minute you entered this world
My life felt complete
And for that I love you.

Dear Sister
Blood or not

I love you forever
And I hope you know that
I love you, Sister!

Nikola Rence (13)
The Ferrers School, Higham Ferrers

Dear Past Self

Dear past self,
Sorry I let you down,
My mum was being a clown.

She pulled my hair
And always swore.

Being sad every day,
That's not okay.

Why would she do this?
I just wanted a kiss.

Nobody should have to go through this.
Always speak up, never give up
Because I'm okay now,
You're probably thinking how?

I'm with my dad,
Now I'm not sad.

I feel grateful for my parents,
Because they aren't careless.

I feel so proud,
I'm okay now.

My life has gotten better,
I wish it could have been sooner.

Now I see my mum,
It is now fun.

Remember,
Always speak up,
Never give up.

Kacie-Leigh Sherwood (11)
The Ferrers School, Higham Ferrers

My School

The time and effort I put within will always put me higher.
The bonds and memories that are made will always make me smile.

The support the teachers give will always keep me going.
My family always bringing motivation is what keeps me trying.

The work that I put in will always help me for my big tests before I leave.
When that time is here when I leave the school I will for sure bring some tears.

The thoughts and feelings that are brought,
The thought of my report, will I pass or be one mark short?
The future is only to know.

Sat on the field with my friends the happiness that is brought.
Ring, ring! goes the bell, time for my next class.

Maisy Lord (12)
The Ferrers School, Higham Ferrers

Dear Future Me

Dear future me
Don't do anything stupid
Don't make bad choices
Just be you.

Dear future me
Do well at school
Get along with your teachers
And feel free.

Dear future me
Don't be afraid to put yourself out there
Don't be judged for who you are
And be the person you hope to be.

Dear future me
Every day walk out the door
With a smile on your face
Don't stop believing.

Dear future me
Treat others fairly
Be there for them as well as yourself
And never turn back.

Dear future me
Live up to your hopes and dreams
Even if you have to run a marathon.

Maddy Slater (12)
The Ferrers School, Higham Ferrers

To The People Who Panic

To the people who panic,
Life will be okay.
Smile and enjoy the flowers
And ignore the bad days.

We won't be here forever,
So enjoy life while you can,
Imagine you are on a peaceful beach,
With a fan.

To the people who panic,
I understand how you feel,
But don't worry how the day will go
Before your breakfast meal!

The days go by and then the weeks,
Yet all we do is worry.
You care so much for everyone else
But you need to make time for yourself.

To the people who panic,
You are perfect the way you are
And don't ever let anyone change your mind.

Izzy Greco (13)
The Ferrers School, Higham Ferrers

Being Weird Is Okay

This poem is weird and so are you!
You want to know how?
Well 10 times out of 10 you're different.
You act differently from the person next to you.
To add a touch bit more weirdness you could read the poem how you like.
Read it upside down or backwards!
Anyway, here's the weirdest poem you'll ever read.

I 'm weird and so is everyone.
M y favourite YouTuber is weird.

W e are all weird in our own way.
E ven you are weird.
I f nobody was weird we would all be the same.
R ight or wrong? Who cares!
D ogs are weird too (especially mine).

Jack Spackman (12)
The Ferrers School, Higham Ferrers

Everything And Nothing

When I was younger, I wanted everything.
Money, clothes, food, games.
The things that everyone had.
Maybe if I did then they'd quit calling me names.
I had my family, but they weren't enough for me.
If I had more, maybe I'd be less sad.

Now I'm older, I have everything.
Money, clothes, food, games.
Things that everyone wants.
People admire me, worship me, despise me.
But they have so much more than I'll ever have.
Companions, friends, family,
All the people they're so prepared to abandon,
Just like me, before I lost mine.
Now I have everything and nothing at all.

Nicola Bartlett (13)
The Ferrers School, Higham Ferrers

My Idol

You have inspired me so much.
You listen to my thoughts and feelings.
You lift me up when I'm at my hardest times.
You let me be myself.
You make me so much happier.
You make me feel me every day.
You have made me feel so much more myself.
You let me not become a different person but make me unique.
You have wiped so many tears off my face when I'm upset.
This is all to say thank you so much for what you have done for me and helping me through tough times.
I am so grateful that you have been by my side through everything.
I have had my up and my down days and you have helped me through them all.

Millie Pears (12)
The Ferrers School, Higham Ferrers

Be Strong. Be Brave. Be You

The bullies come up, you walk away.
They scream and shout, you take another step.
Be strong. Be brave. Be you.

They find you online and have a good laugh.
You figure it out and shut it all down.
Be strong. Be brave. Be you.

You try and live your life but they are still there.
They push you and shove you but you let them.
Be strong. Be brave. Be you.

You feel like a caterpillar but you turn into a butterfly.
They snatch your diary and read it aloud.
Be strong. Be brave. Be you.

Stand up to the bullies.
They probably have a bad life.
Be strong. Be brave. Be you.

Sophia Baxter (11)
The Ferrers School, Higham Ferrers

England's Best Game Yet

England, England, England,
All the fans cheered,
All the tackles made,
All the goals scored,
Thank you, England.

England were ready to score
To stop the fans from getting bored,
The players were inspiring and filled with confidence,
Thank you, England.

England wanted to make the game close,
But the football hit the post,
Thank you, England.

All the fans oohed and aahed,
The fans were nervous because the game was close,
England hit the post,
Thank you, England.

The game finished 2-1 to England
The game was in Finland
Thank you, England.

Joshua Jones (12)
The Ferrers School, Higham Ferrers

Thank You, Mum

Thank you for what you have done
You got me through thick and thin
Through past ups and downs.

I don't know what else I can say but thank you
For staying with me through pain
Able to make me happy through pain.

Thank you for what you have done
Able to give me a roof over my head
To be able to feed me no matter what.

Thank you for everything
Supported me when I was sad
And we had fun together when I was happy.

You have brought me here
And I want to spend as long as I can with you
I want to have fun with you
So thank you Mum for what you have done.

Flynn Bradley-Snell (13)
The Ferrers School, Higham Ferrers

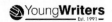

This Is Our World

This is our world
Why are we destroying it?
The lush vibrant rainforests
Cutting them down
Animals losing habitats
For our own selfish needs.

This is our world
Why are we polluting it?
Dumping plastic without a care
Suffocating the fish
Ocean life digesting it
Joining our food chain
Becoming part of us.

This is our world
Why are we choking it?
Filling the air
With poisonous gases
Raising the temperature
Melting the ice caps
Killing our reefs
Leaving creatures powerless.

This is our world
We need to protect it!

Alex Carter (12)
The Ferrers School, Higham Ferrers

Luton On Their Way

At Wembley,
In the final,
Will Luton win?
We show no denial.

At Wembley,
The players can't cope,
But with Nathan Jones
The fans have got hope.

At Wembley,
Adebayo takes the shot,
Will he miss?
I think not.

At Wembley,
The crowd sings his name,
He scores the shot,
To secure Luton's fame.

At Wembley,
The crowd go insane,
They jump onto the pitch,
Still screaming his name.

At Wembley,
He's standing still like a gnome,

He just thought to himself,
This is my home.

Matthew Randall (12)
The Ferrers School, Higham Ferrers

My Future Self

Dear my future self,
Did the world fall off the shelf
Or is it hanging off a piece of cord
That could snap and rub us off the board?
Can the fish still swim
Or have they been replaced with a plastic bin?
And can the bird still fly
Or have they been ruined by plastic in the sky
That's being controlled by the wind?
The world is being heated from within
But also the sun does its thing
But that's not the problem...
It's the humans not trying to save our world from dying,
And that's the reason our world is going down,
But unlike fish it is going to drown.

Alex Billing (13)
The Ferrers School, Higham Ferrers

Ukraine

We all need to change because Ukraine is in pain.
They're screaming for help but no one seems to listen.
Their lungs are full of dust and their tears are all bunched up.
The people of Ukraine are fighting for their lives,
They put up a fight and don't back down.
We hear their voices, we hear them loud,
So please stand up and listen to the voices and pray for Ukraine.
They're losing their homes, they're losing their lives.
They cry themselves to sleep every night.
Some have lost their loved ones.
To this crime Putin's admitted.
Their towns are falling down.

Pippa Mason (11)
The Ferrers School, Higham Ferrers

Football Is For Me

Football is for me
It is everything I want to be
He wears the number seven proud and strong
He passes the ball like he is playing ping pong.

Football is for me
Ronaldo is dribbling along
He skills out everyone
He smashes the ball nice and strong
He has scored a goal
He will do it again
The thrashing of the opponents has just begun.
Suiii!

Football is for me
Now he has a penalty
He dragged his foot along
Bang! He smashed it
He never gets it wrong.

Football is for me
Football is for me
Football is for me!

Zach Jones (12)
The Ferrers School, Higham Ferrers

Inspiration

To the person who inspires me,
You push me, encourage me,
You may not see me or hear me
But I want to say you make me try harder,
So I want to say thank you.

To someone else who inspires me,
You make me train harder,
Train like a tiger and run like a cheetah,
You make me want to sleep all night,
So I want to say thank you.

To the person in my family that inspires me,
You make me feel better,
You reassure me like a newborn baby,
You calm me, you help me
And make me feel grateful for everything God gave me,
So I want to say thank you.

Coen Marks (11)
The Ferrers School, Higham Ferrers

For Supporting Me

Because of you, Brother, pushing me to my limits.
For playing with me on rainy days,
Making me laugh, filling me with joy,
Thanks for everything.

Because of you, Dad, teaching me all your knowledge.
You taught me about power tools and bike riding,
All my success is from your helpful judging,
Thanks for everything.

Because of you, Mum, giving me a shoulder to cry on.
You always fixed my shattered heart,
And baked delicious tarts,
Thanks for everything.

Because you put up with me,
Because you never complained,
Thank you all.

Jamie Gwynne (12)
The Ferrers School, Higham Ferrers

The Perfect Princess

When I was five
I wanted to be a Disney princess.
But as I got older I felt as though I didn't fit the role.
I wasn't perfectly skinny, with a tiny, slim waist,
I didn't have the perfect nose,
I didn't even have the 'right' face with beautiful blue eyes.
But I don't need a small waist
And perfect face, blue eyes,
I am perfectly beautiful with my brave brown eyes.
I am perfect,
I am me,
And because of that I say,
Thank you to my perfect parents.
They helped me realise I am fine how I am.
I am perfect.
I am me.

Chloe Sage
The Ferrers School, Higham Ferrers

A Climate Difference

Oh climate change,
It's sincerely a range of problems in our lives,
Like we're stuck in our bee hives, icebergs crashing down,
Nothing is bound to be going around.
Ice caps melting, as well as us helping,
Scientists are trying when the polar bears are dying.
The ozone is making a bend, but this won't be the end.
The sun is killing us and its heat is just too rough.
Our fossil fuels are doing too much,
While we ain't doing a bunch to stop a lot of countries, like a robot,
This world can't end if we defeat the ozone's bend.

Connor Stephen (11)
The Ferrers School, Higham Ferrers

My Friend Forever

Thank you for being there for me
Through all the ups and downs.
You've stuck by my side like the loyal friend you are.

We've known each other for some time now,
You shine over me with your sun's ray,
Even when I'm not feeling my best,
You'll still be there with me, night till day.

Remember all those times we played together,
Laughing with me by my side,
Like two peas in a pod we were,
Being there for me even when I cried.

Thank you for being my friend forever,
Hope you've enjoyed the ride!

Ann Joseph (13)
The Ferrers School, Higham Ferrers

Reflection

As I stared at myself,
With the lines all drawn of where I think the scissors
Should snip me away.

A perfect waist,
A plastic face,
Big lips injected with poison.

So many things that I wish I could do,
To look exactly like you.

Thoughts flood my head,
All the little voice says,
"All these pretty faces are better than you."

All the time this plays on my mind,
Like little goblins taunting their victims.

The god in my head,
Cloudy and grey,
My thoughts eating away at me.

Tabitha Lipner (13)
The Ferrers School, Higham Ferrers

My Idol

To Tyson Fury,

You inspire me a lot as you are a very strong person physically and mentally.

There are also more reasons.

One of them is your backstory.

You went through a lot of stuff that not many people would have been able to handle.

Whenever I'm feeling down I remember reading about you as you help me mentally.

I also do boxing.

I box at Titan Fitness and my coach says I'm very good for my age.

I hope one day I will be able to meet you and come and watch one of your fights before you retire.

Good luck with all of your fights.

Kai Florez (12)

The Ferrers School, Higham Ferrers

Keeley

When I am in the darkness
Alone in my thoughts
Crying in my pillow
She pulls me out of the darkness nevertheless.

When I am sore from the battle
In the sky I hear a rattle
It is her opening the door from Heaven
Gracefully floating from the amber sky
Like the amazing angel she is.

She is a queen and a leader
And she made me a believer
She is fighting with the world on her shoulders
And yet she still has time for me.

And that is why
You are my best friend
I love you, Keeley.

Niamh Davidson (13)
The Ferrers School, Higham Ferrers

Chasing My Dream Job

C arry on chasing your dreams,
A car mechanic, I
R eally need you to be.

M ake sure you never give up and
E ventually you'll be a role model.
C an you try your best to remember this?
H opefully you are inspired by this.
A ll I can say now is goodbye.
N ever let someone get in your way.
I hope you remember this.
C ar mechanics are the best type of mechanic so keep chasing the job and don't wait for an opportunity... Find an opportunity.

Dylan Glenn (12)
The Ferrers School, Higham Ferrers

Feeling The Win On Stage

Flash!
Lights flashing, music flashing,
People cheering,
You are the happiest person ever!

Don't, don't stop dancing,
You are doing your best,
You might need a rest,
But it is the best.

Don't, don't stop dancing,
Just keep practising,
Practice makes perfect.

Don't, don't stop dancing,
The costumes, the make-up,
The cheering of you winning.

Judges, judging,
Dancers dancing
And most of all,
Happiness spreading.

Maizie Barnes (12)
The Ferrers School, Higham Ferrers

Thanks, Mum

She makes me happy,
She helped me drain all my sadness away
And make me believe in myself,
I love her for that.

She gave me faith,
She gave me respect,
I love her for that.

She is trustworthy,
She is helpful,
I love her for that.

She cared for me when I was up all night being ill,
She fixes my mistakes where I've gone wrong,
I love her for that.

She will always be my idol,
She is the person who inspires me,
For everything she does,
Thank you.

Hollie-Jade Johnstone (13)
The Ferrers School, Higham Ferrers

Axolotls

Axolotls are salamanders from Mexico
Named by the Aztecs so long ago
They live in Xochimilco lake's flow.
Axolotl, the fire and thunder god
He turned into an axolotl to hide
From the sacrifice to gods.
This is an amphibious creature
They have many colours
I bet you'll be staring at them for hours.
Did you know that they are slowly dying?
When I found out I started crying
About 1,200 left in the wild!
The effect is not mild
Because they grow back limbs.
Save axolotls!

Troy Allen (12)
The Ferrers School, Higham Ferrers

Congratulations

Congratulations Year 11,
You have made it.
Congratulations I don't even have to say it.
All 12 long years of learning time,
They really have paid off
But please, please, in the exam hall,
Try not to cough.
Congratulations Year 11,
I hope it all went well
Because when I do it, oh, it's gonna be hell.
The day before the first exam,
Get some medical kits
Because we all know that one kid
Who will catch nits.
And we all know it's cold in there,
Grab some mitts.

George Eales (11)
The Ferrers School, Higham Ferrers

Chances

You gave me life, you gave me a chance
And told me to keep going
And for that, I want to say thank you.

You gave me strength, you gave me power
And I have achieved my goal
And for that, I want to say thank you.

You gave me a home, you helped me with my depression
You saved my life when I was little
And for that, I want to say thank you.

You gave me hope, you taught me new things
You helped me overtake my things
And for that, I want to say thank you.

Bartek Chojecki (13)
The Ferrers School, Higham Ferrers

Spurs' Trophy Cabinet

Spurs' trophy cabinet is empty
Unfortunately we can't win a trophy
Sadly we've never won the Premier League
Because we aren't great
All the chances that we put on a plate we bottle
We will make it if we go full throttle
Our cabinet is dusty
Our trophies are so old they're crusty
We are not glory hunters like Man Utd
We aren't United with trophies because we haven't won any
Football isn't about glory it's about passion and aggression.

Charlie Smith (12)
The Ferrers School, Higham Ferrers

Dear 2035

Dear 2035,
Do you think we will survive?
Sea levels are rising and icebergs are melting.
Coral reefs are dying and no one is helping.
Dear 2035,
Do you think we will survive?
No one sees we need to keep our oceans alive,
This all started back in 1985.
Dear 2035,
Do you think we will survive?
Don't start crying if your fur rug isn't clean,
The endangered list is now 41,415.
Dear 2035,
I have one more thing,
Will it ever get better from here?

Lola Church (11)
The Ferrers School, Higham Ferrers

Climate Catastrophe

Will this ever stop?
Every night I dream about the fact that we might live on Mars,
Will this ever stop?
Animals with rings around their necks, dying because of us.
Will this ever stop?
One day this whole world will be gone.
Will this ever stop?
If your life is worth living, so are their lives,
Will this ever stop?
Tick, tick, tick... The world is gone.
Everyone needs to change their ways.
These things are happening.
These things are happening fast.

Evie Kempson (11)
The Ferrers School, Higham Ferrers

My Prayer

To the people of Ukraine
You will find the light
Your eyes will see glory.

Although you suffer now
Russia will no longer gain
So let's end this petrifying war train.

And our promise to you
Is it will all change.

And to all those lonely people
You do not stand alone.

You will be safe.

So I have one final message...
You can stop Vladimir Putin's vile grasp.

Everybody stands in solidarity with you.

Noah Sears (12)
The Ferrers School, Higham Ferrers

Female Empowerment

Fun, funny, fantastic females!
Females who we look up to,
Females who cared for us,
Females who gave us advice when no one else could,
And today that's what makes me feel empowered.

Fighting for our rights,
Fighting for our power,
Fighting for our children,
Fighting for us,
And today that's what makes me feel empowered.

We have a right,
We have power,
We have each other,
And today that's what makes me feel empowered.

Nicole Benford (13)
The Ferrers School, Higham Ferrers

Empower Ukraine To Win

E mpathy is our engine,
M otivation our driving force,
P oetry our fuel.
O micron Variant our brakes,
W ar is like a car crash,
E xpectations are a flat tyre but
R eligion is what matters.

U nderdogs come out on top.
K yiv is the heart,
R ussia is the disease.
A ttacked without warning,
I ndecisive leaders agree,
N ot humane.
E nd this war for Ukraine.

Tallyn Nesic (12)
The Ferrers School, Higham Ferrers

Like A Tiger

I am not confident.
Like a turtle I like to hide.
I am shy,
I want to be like a tiger,
Brave, mighty, strong, powerful, proud.
I need to be the tiger.
For too long I have been shy like a turtle,
I need to transform,
I need to be brave,
I need to be as confident as a tiger,
I need to stand up for myself,
I need to stand up for others,
To be able to help others,
To be like a tiger.
I cannot give up,
I need to be like a tiger.

Casey Collier (12)
The Ferrers School, Higham Ferrers

Dear Future Me

Dear future me,
Don't be afraid to call your family,
They love you,
You may not know it but they do,
It's true.

Dear future me,
Don't be afraid of the days ahead,
They're just as scary,
Be ready for anything.

Dear future me,
Be strong,
Be brave,
Don't be afraid or scared,
Always smile and be happy.

Dear future me,
Have a loving family,
One that cares.
Never be afraid.

Lauren Hallam (11)
The Ferrers School, Higham Ferrers

The Safety Of Animals

Woof! Woof! Meow! Meow!
There are lots more pet sounds.
Cats, dogs, horses, cows, pigs, lots more animals to name,
What's your favourite pet?

Just imagine if these pets were not alive anymore
Because you are testing and abusing them.
These animals want to live.

Animals are dying because of us,
We need to help them before they are gone.
Donate to animal charities,
Even if it's one pound,
Just support them!

Kaylea France (11)
The Ferrers School, Higham Ferrers

Lily Remember

Lily remember,
When I saw you in December.

Lily remember,
When we went shopping
To get you fish.

Lily remember,
When I gave you
Your favourite dish.

Lily remember,
You escaped with the fly
So I started to cry
And I baked some pie.

Lily remember,
When we watched Netflix
And made some bread mix.

Lily remember,
We had a lot of memories
We've been friends for centuries.

Robert Ciachura (13)
The Ferrers School, Higham Ferrers

Sisterly Love

You've always been there for me
Even when I'm in a puddle of tears
And even though we've had our ups and downs.

You're the sister that I've always needed.
You know when I'm in the wrong
Or just the victim.
You've inspired me so.

I never thought that I could have a sister like you.
You are my hero.
You and me are blood.
You are the best sister I could wish for.
You are my one and only sister.

Lilly Peer (12)
The Ferrers School, Higham Ferrers

Ukraine Support

U nder pressure from the Russians
K illing the invaders
R ussians dying every day
A ttacking back
I nside Ukraine
N ot giving up
E mpowering Ukrainian soldiers

S upporting lives
U kraine's winning
P lanes protecting their country
P utin's losing
O ld places are lost to bombs
R efugees finding safety
T oday I back my country.

Finley Roberts (12)
The Ferrers School, Higham Ferrers

No More

I hate the way you feel the need to tell me what to wear.
I hate the way I'm minding my own business and men just stop and stare.
I hate the way I'm discriminated against for my gender and nothing more.
I hate the way I'm constantly called a s*** or w****.
I hate the way you have control over me no matter the situation and I never get credit.
I hate how I'm an object to you.
I hate how I'm treated as something less.
I hate it all.

Lucy Gay (13)
The Ferrers School, Higham Ferrers

What Does Music Mean To Me?

Music is why everyone breathes,
It's why the wind sways in the trees.
It helps people wander along free,
Whisked away with the sound of the beat.

Imagine a world with no music,
How would the world run free?
What would make us dance or fill our bodies with glee?
Music is why everyone breathes.

Never will I let you go,
Even when it's to or fro.
No matter when the world is gone,
Music will be there all along.

Verity Kent (13)
The Ferrers School, Higham Ferrers

My Sisters

To my sisters,
Even though we fight
And after, make it right, I love you.
To my influencer,
You made me who I am,
And I love you for that.
To my best friends,
I could tell you anything
And you wouldn't judge.
To my favourite two girls,
You were the first two girls who were there for me,
You were the first two girls I argued with.
To my sisters,
You put a smile on my face
And I will always love you for that.

Carly Smith (11)
The Ferrers School, Higham Ferrers

Global Warming

Global warming is killing,
Global warming is destroying
And it's all our fault.

Cars, buses and planes powered by fuel,
Making weak spots for the sun to take advantage.

Animals are losing their homes,
Animals are dying, Antarctica is melting.

Soon there will be no Antarctica,
Soon there will be no polar bears,
Soon there will be no life.

Recycle, re-use and help your planet.
Time is ticking.

Kyla Cape (12)
The Ferrers School, Higham Ferrers

Empowered

Push through the pain of life and keep on believing.
Try your hardest and never give up.
Embrace your fears and keep your head up.
Enemies anchor you down but friends help you up.
Life can be rough but love is your prize.
You may want to curl up into a ball and cry
But you need to remember that at the end of the day,
Your family has your back and will love you no matter what.
Shoot for the stars and don't let anything keep you down.

Finley Cleverley (12)
The Ferrers School, Higham Ferrers

Dear Prime Minister

Dear Prime Minister
Have you lost your rhyme?
Can't keep us in time
Kept us in lockdown
While you party
Not so crafty
Ruined 2021
Since you have nothing better to do
Don't ruin 2022
Losing rhyme
Can't keep in time
Lost the war with Covid
Overpowered, lost the structure
It isn't safe for humans now.

Dear Prime Minister
Since you have nothing better to do
Don't ruin 2022!

Dylan Riddell
The Ferrers School, Higham Ferrers

Dear My Past Self

Dear my past self,
I'm here to tell you,
The one who taught you,
'Sticks and stones may break my bones
But words will never hurt me'.
Whose words will hurt the most.

Dear my past self,
I'm here to tell you
The one you love the most
Will be the one to break your heart,
Before any teenage boy could.

Dear my past self,
No matter what Eminem says,
Daddy won't buy you a mockingbird.

Carlie Sharp (13)
The Ferrers School, Higham Ferrers

When I See You

When I see you I fill with hope,
Like a dead person coming back to life.
You're always there when I need you most,
Kind and fun to hang with, we laugh and cry together.
You light up my world when times are worse,
When I see you I feel safe,
When I leave I miss you the most.
You've brought the best out of me,
When I leave I want to go back to you,
When I see you I fill with hope,
Like a dead person coming back to life.

Georgia Goss (12)
The Ferrers School, Higham Ferrers

Dear Me

Dear my past self,
Stay strong when you don't feel it.
Believe in yourself.
Always listen to everything,
You never know when you'll use it.
Dear my past self,
Never give up on yourself.
Love yourself no matter what.
Dear my future self,
Never give up,
You never know what the future holds,
And stand your ground.
Dear my future self,
Never give up and stay strong
And you'll get your dream.

Sydney Neuville (12)
The Ferrers School, Higham Ferrers

Dear Future Me

Dear future me,
What's it like to be me?
Do I look the same
Or do I still look plain?
What's it like to be me?

To my future self,
How is your health?
Are you free or will no one leave you be?
What's it like to be me?

Dear future me,
What's it like to be me?
Are they still there
Or are they someone you can't bear?

Dear future me,
What's it like to be me?

Ellie Cassidy (13)
The Ferrers School, Higham Ferrers

Fish In The Ocean

In the ocean there are fish...
Some are big, some are old,
Some have teeth, some have none,
Some are small, some are young,
Some eat meat, some do not,
Most live in the sea or in the river,
Or the lake down the road.
Some are coloured but some are dull,
Most are silent but some make noise.
But no matter if they are silent or noisy,
Or young or old, or even colourless,
They are all still fish no matter what.

Noah McCrossan (12)
The Ferrers School, Higham Ferrers

Cousin

Thank you for being there for me
So I have a shoulder to cry on,
You helped me when I felt stuck,
And when I thought I had no luck.

12 years and way more to come,
You filled me with confidence and courage,
You helped me when I had no hope,
You helped me learn to cope.

You always find a way,
To make me laugh when I'm sad,
While I'm thinking to myself,
I'm bad, I'm bad!

Mia Beckett (13)
The Ferrers School, Higham Ferrers

Dear Past Me...

Dear past me
A favour that I ask
Happiness doesn't last forever
So please make it last.

Dear past me
A favour that I ask
Spend more time with loved ones
Because it might be your last.

Dear past me
A favour that I ask
Help your sister out
Because friendship never lasts.

Dear past me
The last favour that I ask
Spend your life the fullest
Because life never lasts.

Abigail Wells (12)
The Ferrers School, Higham Ferrers

Like A Bear And Its Cub

Helping me through, when times get tough,
Even though for you it might get rough,
Like a bear and its cub.

You cook, you clean, you help me be me,
And you give me your hand when in need,
Like a bear and its cub.

You give me your life, your faith, your hope and your light,
You help me out of the dumps and give me a smile,
Like a bear and its cub.

To you I'm thankful
My beloved grandad.

Zaibian Andrews (12)
The Ferrers School, Higham Ferrers

To Someone Special To Me

She's special to me,
She was by my side from the day I was born,
And thanks to you I'm who I am today.

She's special to me,
She would always make sure we were happy,
And did her best every hour of the day.
And thanks to you I'm who I am today.

She's special to me,
She supports me and I support her
And comforted me when our pets died.
And thanks to you I'm who I am today.

Brianna Furniss (13)
The Ferrers School, Higham Ferrers

Don't Leave It

Dear past me,
Don't go to school today,
Don't move house,
Don't wish on a miracle.

Dear past me,
Have all the fun you can,
Have all the happiness you can get,
Have the best nine years you can.

Dear past me,
Enjoy every last moment you have,
Enjoy all the celebrations,
Enjoy all the things you get.

Fear future me,
Stay powered,
Stay ready,
Stay there.

Mansher Shetra (12)
The Ferrers School, Higham Ferrers

Am I Not Enough?

I wanted to win,
I wanted to beat my friends,
Maybe then they would appreciate me more.
All I was to them was the second choice,
I was trapped in a friend group and in this stupid maze!

I wanted to win,
The only way to win was to escape.
Escape this mess,
Escape this maze.
Maybe then I would finally have motivation
And finally be happy.
If only this could happen.
If only I was brave enough.

Sophie Watson (13)
The Ferrers School, Higham Ferrers

To Dad - Happy Birthday

You have helped me through times good and bad,
Cheered me up when I was sad.
Done everything with me and I'm really glad.
From a very lucky son, happy birthday, Dad.

You give me confidence, memories and fun,
How much do I love you? I love you a tonne.
Since day one, we have gelled like glue,
And I just want to say, thank you.

Have the best of birthdays,
To the best dad I could wish for.

Josh Pocock (13)
The Ferrers School, Higham Ferrers

Body Images

I hate it.
The feeling of sadness weighs me down like an anchor.
The best even feels like the worst.
I slump on the sofa once more.
The stone is sinking in the river.
The over-enthusiastic TV presenter for Pointless was cut off by a work out act.
I have never felt this motivated.
This ugly duckling will be a swan
And I felt empowered to make this dream come true.
That is what I will put myself through.

Olivia Messiou (12)
The Ferrers School, Higham Ferrers

Dear Future Me

Dear future me,
Don't give up on football.
Don't be afraid to take risks.
Don't forget your family.
Dear future me,
Don't be scared to try new things.
Don't leave your friends.
Don't be scared to ask for help.
Dear future me,
Please know that everything will work out.
Please stay loyal.
Please take care of your family.
Dear future me,
Please stay being me.

Logan Fowler (12)
The Ferrers School, Higham Ferrers

The Earth

Day by day the Earth goes round
And it supplies us with all our needs.

But still we spoil its treasures with all our rubbish,
Scourging the seas with our plastic bottles
And polluting our skies with our carbon emissions
And destroying land and animals with our wars.

To think that this world was once a paradise, now gone.
To think we deserve this world after what we have done,
We are wrong.

Harry Baker (12)
The Ferrers School, Higham Ferrers

Our British Coasts And How To Look After Them

Have you ever felt like getting away?
Maybe for a week or maybe just a day,
We can always count on our British seaside,
Home to amusements, fish and chips and sealife.
We all love a nice picnic on the beach,
But there's also a negative side to it
And I'll tell you why with my little speech...

Every day our oceans are polluted more,
The litter we leave behind is washed out from the shore.

Madison Lewis (13)
The Ferrers School, Higham Ferrers

My Home

You keep me warm when it's cold
You protect me from the weather
You gift me a place to sleep
You shelter me from all things bad
You give me safety
You keep me safe
You are big
You are strong
You make me feel safe
Without you I am cold
Without you I am unsafe
Without you I am scared
When you are with me I am happy
When you are with me I feel empowered
You are my home.

Mike Rainsley (12)
The Ferrers School, Higham Ferrers

Happy Birthday

Amazing, kind and caring,
Those are the words that describe you
And I hope you know it too.

Happy birthday, Jack,
You have a lot to unwrap
Because today is a special day.

You have always been there
And always seem to care,
So have a great day, it's all about you.

Funny, cheerful and bright,
Those are the words that describe you
And I hope you know it too.

Sophie O'Connor (12)
The Ferrers School, Higham Ferrers

Song

Dear people,
You take and don't give back.
You steal, you thieve.
You cut, you hack.
Dear people,
We wish you saw the damage.
We wish you saw the heartbreak.
We wish you saw the death.
Dear people,
I hope we get justice.
I hope you're sorry
But I hope one day we forgive
For all the selfish things you did.
Dear people,
I hope one day we're equal.

Olivia Hall (13)
The Ferrers School, Higham Ferrers

Gone, But Not Forgotten

The world carries on,
But he's paused in pain.
Thoughts bouncing around in his head,
Trying to escape.
Gone, but still remembered.

No other way to escape,
But then to leave.
This cruel world was too much to handle.
Gone, but still loved.

God gave a strong person,
A tough life for him,
He thought this was his only escape.
Gone, but not forgotten.

Sophie Gumbrecht (13)
The Ferrers School, Higham Ferrers

Invasion

About 30 odd years ago the Soviets broke away,
There was always anguish.
Why? There is no need for war,
Let's bring peace to this world.

They crept into their land
With a gun in their hand,
Ready to raid the towns.
Can we turn back the time?

I wish it could all stop
But the fighting goes on,
With brave, brave men and women
Fighting for their country.

Tom Ford (12)
The Ferrers School, Higham Ferrers

Empower Yourself

E njoy your education.
M ental health. Take care of it.
P ower. Have power over yourself.
O wn your life decisions.
W orried. If you're worried take action.
E nvironment. Show love for the environment.
R ights. Value our human rights.
E xpress your emotions.
D on't allow anything to stop you from achieving your dreams.

Molly Parr (11)
The Ferrers School, Higham Ferrers

Where I Feel Alive

Out on the road, as the cars fly by,
That's where I feel alive.
Out in the country, with the peachy sky winking,
And the sound of birds chirping,
That's where I feel alive.
Out by the ocean,
With the waves stroking the shore and clean air blowing,
That's where I feel alive.
Out on the road,
With the thought of coming home,
That's where I feel alive.

Owen Williams (12)
The Ferrers School, Higham Ferrers

My Idol

The crowd screams and chants,
Shouting, "Harry Kane! Harry Kane! Harry Kane!" with excitement.
The speediness of the players is fascinating to see,
The skills twirling and whirling
And Harry Kane headers it in with a hat-trick.
The whole crowd chanting to Heaven
With excitement from the players
It's unbelievable, Spurs have won again.

Harrison Eaton-Clark (12)
The Ferrers School, Higham Ferrers

Empowerment

E ducation
M oney
P owerless to become powerful
O wnership
W orth giving power to others and yourself
E ncouraging other people to gain confidence
R esponsibilities
M aking decisions
E veryone supports each other
N ever give up
T herapists to help with problems.

Ruby Douglas (12)
The Ferrers School, Higham Ferrers

Stop Bullying

St **O** p
o **N** line
Bul **L** ying
I t's
importa **N** t
To **E** nsure

B ut we need
yo **U** to
he **L** p
a **L** ot
Y ou should help
today **I** n schools
N ot when it's too late
G o into schools and give a speech to stop bullying

Millie Catterill (12)
The Ferrers School, Higham Ferrers

The Sound Of Instruments

Dear my future self,
Did the brass fall off its shelf?
And do the notes still play in time?
Does the uke still play its chime
Or does it sound like a crime?
One thing that I ask of you
Is that you can make this poem rhyme
Or perhaps you keep the piano's chime
Or the bass still gives you a rush of the sublime.

Liam Rushton (13)
The Ferrers School, Higham Ferrers

Courage

Sturdy yet fast
You jump a 1200-pound beast over a 5-foot jump
You fall
"Get up! Get up!"
Silence... You get up, hop on and try again
You succeed
You have courage
Flashing lights
Flashing cameras
Flashing gold and red first place rosette
So next time you fall, get up and get back on.

Katelyn Abbott (12)
The Ferrers School, Higham Ferrers

Hunter The Husky

You make me happy,
You make me mad,
But no matter what, I love you.
And when you pull on walks,
Even when you try and attack me,
I still love you,
Even when you dribble your water everywhere,
Even when you chase the birds around,
Even when you wake me up at five in the morning,
I still love you.

Preston Bedford (12)
The Ferrers School, Higham Ferrers

My Love

I came into this world not knowing who
I came into this world, just me and you
13 years of loving you
13 years of me and you.

When I am in a bad place
You always help me
Even if I made a bad mistake
And I always talk to you
If anyone is on my case.

I want to say thank you.

Hemi Drage (13)
The Ferrers School, Higham Ferrers

Empowered

What is it
That makes you feel empowered?

Being mean? Being nice?
Making people cry? Making people laugh?

Or winning a competition?
Maybe a race?

Is it just participating
Knowing someone is happy.

And so,
What is it
That makes you feel empowered?

Roman Dangerfield-Simons (12)
The Ferrers School, Higham Ferrers

The Ukraine Fighters

In Ukraine they are fighting
With the world by their side
They might fall but they stand up and be their best
Russia keeps fighting, but we go on.

In Ukraine they are fighting
Homes are lost
Lives are gone.

In Ukraine
We support all those
That are gone.

Ollie Smith (12)
The Ferrers School, Higham Ferrers

If I Was The Prime Minister For One Day I Would...

If I was the prime minister for one day
I would make a day called Bettles Day
And then I would make taxes cheaper
And make a day where taxes and bills were free.
I would make schools more fun for kids
Then I'd meet the Queen, have a chat
And let her do what she wants.

Noah Bettles (12)
The Ferrers School, Higham Ferrers

Football

The power, the energy,
The confidence on that pitch.
The friendship, the skills
Boosts my energy up like a star.
The passion in that game lights me up.
The skills on the ball
Boosts my mental health.
The talks within the team
Boosts my confidence and energy.

Max Walker (12)
The Ferrers School, Higham Ferrers

Sunny Days

The sun shone through my window,
I could feel the hot breeze from the sun.
The sun helps me rest all the time,
Sunny days are the best.

The sound of the birds chirping,
The sound of kids playing,
The sound of the ice cream van,
Sunny days are the best.

Chloe Newman (12)
The Ferrers School, Higham Ferrers

Dear Mum

Dear Mum
You have been there through thick and thin,
Day after day.

Dear Mum
You have been there since day one
Tears and cheers.

Dear Mum
You have been there since I was young.

Dear Mum
You have been there through it with me.

Scarlett Hanscombe (12)
The Ferrers School, Higham Ferrers

My Favourite Things About Me

I like my hair because it's a really nice shade.
It's a blonde-brown hair shade.
It reminds me of the silk of covers and pillows.

I like the shade of my eyes,
They are a blue and green,
The colour reminds me of the sea swishing forwards and backwards.

Alexia Newman (12)
The Ferrers School, Higham Ferrers

Self-Love

Don't let that person with the frown get you down
Don't let it ruin your day
Go put on that fabulous gown
And live your life day by day.

Yes you might feel sad
Yes you might be mad
But that is not all bad
Just treasure what you have.

Emilia Denne (13)
The Ferrers School, Higham Ferrers

Arsenal

A tmosphere surrounds the stadium
R eading the scoreline
S coring against our rivals
E mirates Stadium is our home
N ew signings every summer
A bove 5th in the table
L ooking down at the game in the stadium.

Isaac Bennett (13)
The Ferrers School, Higham Ferrers

Football

Football is good,
It's good for fitness
And for mental health.
It's a fantastic hobby
That brings people together.
Family and friends chatting
About the beautiful game,
The crowd go wild,
The goal rattles,
Glory and passion.

Ashley Batterley (13)
The Ferrers School, Higham Ferrers

My Love

You are loved a lot
So don't think you're not
Stop wasting your time
And come be mine.

You're my hope, you're my home
Without you I'm nothing.
So come back, with no lack
And be mine for the rest of time.

Amelia Grieves (13)
The Ferrers School, Higham Ferrers

Ocean Plastic

O asis shimmering in the sun.
C ongested with plastic polluting the water.
E xpected to wipe out fish by 2050.
A species, gone forever.
N ature's loss.
S erved up from our foolishness.

Hendrix Smyth (12)
The Ferrers School, Higham Ferrers

Dream Come True

The crowd erupted with cheers,
The dribbling blue sky was clear.
Walking through the light tunnel,
Sweating like water through a funnel.
Whistle blown,
Everyone unknown.
Ball at my feet,
Couldn't hear a peep.

Adam Newman (13)
The Ferrers School, Higham Ferrers

He Was On The Pitch

He was on the pitch
Everyone was relieved
We all believed.

He was on the pitch
Of course he will score
His ability never bores.

He was on the pitch
We all admired
We were all inspired.

Isaac Hemmington (13)
The Ferrers School, Higham Ferrers

My Best Friends

My best friends...
The people who brighten up my mood,
Who cheer me up when I'm blue.

My best friends...
The people who make me laugh a little bit harder,
Brighten up my day and make me smile.

Olivia Mitchell (11)
The Ferrers School, Higham Ferrers

Friends

Your worries are mine,
My worries are yours.

You're my place to go when I want to feel safe,
Who I talk to when someone is on my case.

Forever me and you,
Forever me and you.

Zara Boot (12)
The Ferrers School, Higham Ferrers

Bella My Dog

B eautiful doggy
E xcellent companion
L ovely snout
L uscious fur
A mazing tail.

Charlie Adams (13)
The Ferrers School, Higham Ferrers

YoungWriters Est. 1991

YOUNG WRITERS INFORMATION

We hope you have enjoyed reading this book – and that you will continue to in the coming years.

If you're the parent or family member of an enthusiastic poet or story writer, do visit our website **www.youngwriters.co.uk/subscribe** and sign up to receive news, competitions, writing challenges and tips, activities and much, much more! There's lots to keep budding writers motivated!

If you would like to order further copies of this book, or any of our other titles, then please give us a call or order via your online account.

Young Writers
Remus House
Coltsfoot Drive
Peterborough
PE2 9BF
(01733) 890066
info@youngwriters.co.uk

Join in the conversation!
Tips, news, giveaways and much more!

YoungWritersUK YoungWritersCW youngwriterscw